know
the
game

D0433267

NETBALL

Produced in collaboration with the
All England Netball Association

Published by A & C Black (Publishers) Ltd
35 Bedford Row, London WC1R 4JH

Foreword

Netball has become a popular international sport and its rules of play are under the control of the International Federation of Netball Associations. This new edition of Know the Game Netball incorporates amendments to the rules made by the International Federation in Singapore in June 1983.

Rena Stratford is an internationally respected authority on Netball. She played a leading role in the formation of the International Federation in 1960 and served as its Organising Secretary and President, as well as holding office as the National Technical Officer and President of the All England Netball Association for many years. She was the writer of the first edition of Know the Game Netball which has proved to be an extremely valuable aid to many thousands of players, coaches and umpires.

With her unique qualifications, Miss Stratford has brought this latest edition up to date and I have much pleasure in commending it to all those who wish to improve their knowledge and understanding of the rules and basic skills of the game of Netball.

ANNETTE CAIRNCROSS
President
All England Netball Association

SECTION ONE: **The Game**

Netball is an international sport. It is played between two teams of seven players—three of which are forwards or attackers and named Wing Attack, Goal Attack and Goal Shooter; one is the player positioned in the middle called the Centre; and three are backs or defenders and are named Wing Defence, Goal Defence and Goal Keeper.

The aim of the game is to score goals. A goal is scored when the ball is thrown over and through a ring on the top of the goal post from within the attacking team's shooting circle. Only two of the attackers, namely Goal Attack and Goal Shooter, may enter the shooting circle and throw goals.

To start the game or restart it after a goal the ball is thrown off by the Centre from the centre circle and then passed from player to player until it can be caught in the goal circle by one of the two goal-scoring players, who then throws for goal.

The defending team aim to obtain possession of the ball and then attack their goal at the opposite end in the same way.

The Rules of Netball

Because of existing anomalies in the Code of Rules, and the large number of questions on interpretation of the wording being repeatedly received since 1967, the International Rules Sub-Committee decided to re-write the Code of Rules in such a way that it would be easily understood—especially by those countries where English was not the official language. In 1975 the Council agreed that changes were necessary to the rules and presentation to make the code both more logical and more easily understood. The 1975 Code was operated over the next 8 years.

In June 1983 at the Federation's Conference proposals for rule changes came before the Council and a new Code was agreed, which will operate until 1991.

The changes to the game are minimal. However, the changes in the order in which rules are written and the changes in layout should make the details contained in each rule more easily noted and understood by players, umpires and coaches alike.

Rule 1

The Court

The surface

As the surface of the court greatly affects the speed of the game it is best played on a court with a hard surface. A porous, tarmacadam, or asphalt surface is the most suitable, being neither slippery nor holding puddles. Hard rolled hot or cold ash, concrete or wood are also suitable surfaces. A loose top dressing should be avoided, since it is difficult to land safely from a jump. Although in some countries it is possible to play the game on a grass surface, in England grass is most unsatisfactory, and should only be permitted in an emergency.

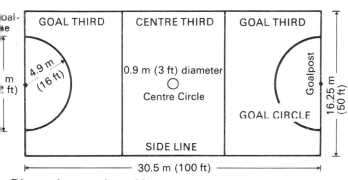

GOAL THIRD | CENTRE THIRD | GOAL THIRD

4.9 m (16 ft)

0.9 m (3 ft) diameter
Centre Circle

Goalpost

GOAL CIRCLE

SIDE LINE

16.25 m (50 ft)

30.5 m (100 ft)

Dimensions and marking

Length: 30.45 m (100 ft)   Width: 15.25 m (50 ft)

The two long lines are called side lines; the two short lines are called goal lines The court is divided down the side lines by two transverse lines into three equal thirds, named centre third and goal thirds.

Goal circles A semi-circle in each goal third; centre, middle of goal line; radius 4.9 m (16 ft).

Centre circle Circle drawn in the middle of the centre third. Diameter 0.9 m (3 ft).

The court, thirds and circles are marked clearly with lines. Lines must not be more than two inches wide. They should be painted with a hard wearing paint or, if temporary, with whitewash or distemper, or by laying adhesive tape.

The width of the side lines and the goal lines are included in the above measurements, for the whole court; the width of

the circle lines is included in the radii of the circles and the width of the transverse lines is common to both adjacent areas.

Equipment

Goalposts

A goalpost of 3.05 m (10 ft) high is placed at the midpoint of each goal line, neither in front nor behind the line. (see over)

The ring has a diameter of 380 mm (15 in). The material of which the ring is constructed is laid down; it shall be of tubular steel and shall be 15 mm ($\frac{5}{8}$ in) in diameter and fitted with a net open at both ends. The ring must project horizontally 150 mm (6 in) from the top of the post. The attachment must allow six inches between the post and the near side of the ring.

The post shall be 65 mm (2.5 in) to 100 mm (4 in) in diameter or up to 100 mm (4 in) square.

The goalpost may be inserted in a socket in the ground or may be supported by a metal base which shall not project on the court. (N.B. the 'mushroom' base which does project on the court no longer fulfils the conditions laid down.)

Manufacturers have their own alternative bases which are legitimate, and some incorporate wheels on the base so that the post may easily be pushed from the court into store. Posts can be found which are jointed; these can be stowed away in the boot of a car.

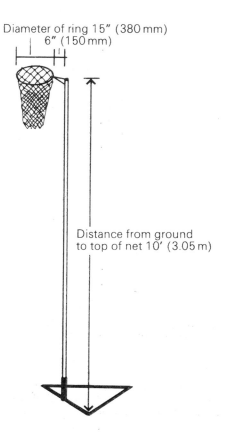

Diameter of ring 15" (380 mm)
6" (150 mm)

Distance from ground
to top of net 10' (3.05 m)

The ball

The ball used is a Netball or size 5 Association Football and measures between 690 mm (27 in) and 710 mm (28 in) in circumference and weighs between 400 g (14 oz) and 450 g (16 oz). The ball may be made of leather, rubber or similar material.

The All England Netball Association officially approves of the Mitre Mouldmaster ball, a moulded rubber ball which fulfils the requirements and is comparatively cheap, very hard-wearing and maintains its size and weight with wear. Most balls nowadays are laceless and therefore easier to inflate and less likely to puncture.

The ball should be kept well inflated—so that when firm pressure is applied through the thumbs and fingers there is very little indentation.

Players' uniform

Registered playing uniforms, which shall include initials of playing positions, shall be worn at all times. Playing initials shall be worn both front and back above the waist and shall be 200 mm (8 in) high.

Shirt or blouse

This should be plain, neat and made of an absorbent material and uniform for the whole team. It should be sufficiently long to tuck into the skirt without becoming untucked when jumping and stretching.

Skirts, shorts or tunic

These should be of uniform colour, style, material and length.

Socks

Socks should be worn; they soak up perspiration and act as shock absorbers. In cold weather tights are suitable for match play, or tracksuit bottoms.

Shoes or boots

Either shoes or boots may be worn. Shoes are individual to each player. The only rules laid down are that they must be made of lightweight material and spiked soles are not allowed.

The players should consider the fit of the shoes, especially round the ankle; 'tennis' shoes with canvas tops and rubber soles are worn by many players, while others prefer a 'training shoe' with leather top and rubber, or other non-slip material, for the sole.

Place 'bibs'

The rules state that playing uniform must include initials of playing positions to be worn at all times. Playing initials must

be worn both on the front and the back above the waist. The letters must be 200 mm (8 in) high.

Jewellery

The rules ban the wearing of all items of jewellery during play. This includes ear-rings, fancy hair slides and combs. It is not a suitable occasion and can be dangerous to other players. No rings may be worn, except a wedding ring, and if a wedding ring is worn it must be taped.

Fingernails must be cut short.

The game is a team game and the uniform a team affair; therefore each individual has a responsibility towards her team members and the opposition. An apology should always be made to the captains and the umpires if, in some emergency, a player's uniform is not complete.

Rule 2

Duration of the Game

A game shall consist of four quarters of fifteen minutes each, with an interval of three minutes between the first and second quarters and the third and fourth quarters and a maximum of ten minutes at half-time.

The captain of each team must tell the umpire what length of half-time her team would like. Should one captain request five minutes and the other ten minutes, then the mean time, or average of the times requested (e.g. in the times given the mean time will be seven and a half minutes) shall determine the length of the half-time interval.

An interval may be extended by the umpires to deal with any emergency. Teams shall change ends each quarter.

Where any team plays two or more matches in one day, as in a 'three-cornered contest' or a tournament, the game shall consist of two halves of twenty minutes each with a maximum five-minute interval at half-time. Again the mean time as requested by the respective teams shall determine the length of the half-time interval. Teams shall change ends at half-time.

The same length of match is also laid down where time is limited, i.e. two halves of twenty minutes.

At elementary level the game can legitimately be shortened even more if the disadvantages are balanced by the gaining of experience in meeting more teams.

At higher levels a ten-minute period of play in each of two halves gives little opportunity or practice in reading the opposing side's play, and of thinking how to counter it.

Time lost for an accident or any other cause must be signalled by the umpire to the timekeeper, noted on the score sheet, and added to that quarter or half of the game. In no case shall extra time be allowed except to take a penalty pass or shot.

In certain climatic conditions the duration of the game shall be pre-determined by the countries concerned.

Rule 3

Officials

The game officials are umpires, scorers and timekeepers.

Team officials are coach, manager and captain.

At international matches all umpires, official scorers and official timekeepers shall be women.

The Umpires

An umpire shall wear a costume distinct from that of the players and, for international play, the costume should preferably be white or cream in colour.

In some countries, umpires at all levels wear white.

The rules state that there shall be two umpires who shall:

a. have control of the game
b. give decisions
c. umpire according to the rules
d. decide on any matter not covered by the rules.

Each umpire shall control and give decisions only in one half of the court unless appealed to by the other umpire for a decision in her half, and be ready for such an appeal.

The decisions of the umpires are FINAL and given WITHOUT APPEAL

Umpires are human and subject to human failings. However good and highly qualified they might be, the umpire will make mistakes. It always has been and, it is hoped, always will be the game's strength that it is accepted that every player respects this rule and accepts the umpire's decisions, even if the player is sure the decision is wrong.

The umpire's whistle shall start and stop the game. Starting, or re-starting the game after a goal or interval shall be controlled by the umpire into whose half the play is to be directed.

After the players have taken their positions on court in preparation for the start of the game, the two umpires shall toss a coin to determine which goal end each shall take.

The umpire winning the toss shall control that half of the court designated the northern half.

Umpire's area of operation

Umpire X gives decisions in the shaded half of the court throughout the game. Her area of operation is limited to this area, of half the court; for this purpose the length of the court is divided in half across the centre circle from side line to side line.

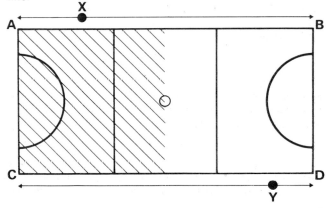

Umpire X restarts the game after all goals scored in her half of the court.

Umpire X also gives decisions for the throw-in for the whole of one side line AB and the goal line AC which bounds her area. She shall call play, when all other players are on court.

She is also responsible for making decisions relating to infringements by the player throwing-in and the defending opponents.

Similarly umpire Y gives decisions in the unshaded area of the court, for the whole length of side line CD and goal line DB for the throw in, and restarts the game after all goals scored in her half of the court.

Movement of umpires

Each umpire shall keep outside the court except when it is necessary to secure a clear view of play or to indicate the place where a penalty is taken or to take a toss-up.

When play moves towards the other end of the court she should follow it down to the end of her territory in line with the centre circle.

She may move further along the side line in the other umpire's half to indicate the place from which a throw-in is to be taken.

Each umpire must move along the sideline and behind the goal-line to observe play in the circle and to make decisions.

Each umpire shall refrain from blowing the whistle to penalise an infringement when, by so doing, the *non-offending* team would be placed at a disadvantage.

An umpire may call '*Advantage*' to indicate that an infringement has been observed and not penalised. If she has blown the whistle for such an infringement, the penalty must be given.

This is commonly known as 'playing the advantage rule.' The advantage rule is quite difficult for inexperienced umpires to understand and difficult for even experienced umpires always to implement. (see Examples A and B.)

The umpire shall:

1. not criticise or *coach* any team or player while a match is in progress.
2. check that during a stoppage for injury or illness, players shall remain on court. During this stoppage no coaching is permitted.
3. on seeing an infringement blow the whistle, state the infringement and penalty, and indicate the place at which the penalty shall be taken.

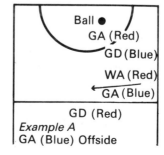

GD (Red)
Example A
GA (Blue) Offside

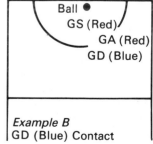

Example B
GD (Blue) Contact

Example A

Red GA has caught the ball and is inside the goal circle. Blue GA has run offside over the transverse line.

Umpire's Correct Decision: Play the Advantage Rule and allow game to go on.

Umpire's Incorrect Decision: Penalise Blue GA—blow whistle and award free pass to Red Team from where Blue GA is offside.

Result: Red GA loses the chance to score.

Example B

Red GS has the ball inside the goal circle and close to goalpost. Blue GD contacts her opponent on the goal circle edge.

Umpire's Correct Decision: Play Advantage Rule and allow GS to make almost certain score.

Umpire's Incorrect Decision: Blow whistle, award a penalty pass to Red Team on the edge of the goal circle.

Result: Red Shooter must either pass or take a harder shot for Goal.

The question is sometimes asked—what if in B, for example, the Umpire plays the Advantage Rule and allows play to continue, but GS fails to score the goal? This can only be answered by saying that the advantage due to Red Team was given. If that advantage was not converted—that is a failure on the part of the Red Team.

Miscellaneous hints to umpires

The umpire no longer has to prepare a score card.

Before the game starts the umpire must give her directions to the scorer and necessary information:
(i)   names of teams taking part in the match;
(ii) which team is to have first centre pass.

The umpire can ask the scorer to check centre passes, and to call it, if she has made a mistake. However, the **responsibility** for the centre pass lies with the umpire. She should find a simple way of remembering that the pass is taken alternately throughout the game without having to be cluttered with paper and pencil. Some umpires use a signet ring which they place on one hand for one team; as soon as a goal is scored, or as soon as the centre pass is taken, she changes it to the other hand.

A coin changed from one pocket to another is another solution. These two examples can stimulate ideas for what would be easy for you. The score does not matter it is only keeping the alternate pass.

If you have difficulties, then ask the scorer to keep you informed.

Scorers

There shall be two scorers who shall:

a.   Keep a written record of the score.
b.   Keep a written record of the centre passes.
c.   Keep a written record of all unsuccessful shots.

d. Record each goal as it is scored (unless notified to the contrary by the umpire — this is the official score of the game.
e. Keep a record of all unsuccessful shots.
f. Call the centre pass if appealed to by the umpire.
g. Notify the umpire immediately if the incorrect centre pass is given.

A sample of an official score sheet

TEAMS	1st QUARTER					2nd QUARTER					3rd QUARTER					4th QUARTER				
CENTRE PASS		GS	GA	GS	GA	CENTRE PASS	GS	GA	GS	GA	CENTRE PASS	GS	GA	GS	GA	CENTRE PASS	GS	GA	GS	GA
ATTEMPTS																				
SCORED																				
QR. SCORE																				
PROGRESSIVE SCORE																				

TEAM _____

1	2	3	4	5	6	7	8	9	10
11	12	13	14	15	16	17	18	19	20
21	22	23	24	25	26	27	28	29	30
31	32	33	34	35	36	37	38	39	40
41	42	43	44	45	46	47	48	49	50
51	52	53	54	55	56	57	58	59	60
61	62	63	64	65	66	67	68	69	70
71	72	73	74	75	76	77	78	79	80
81	82	83	84	85	86	87	88	89	90
91	92	93	94	95	96	97	98	99	100

GOAL SHOOTER
ATTEMPTS:
SCORED:

GOAL ATTACK
ATTEMPTS:
SCORED:

TEAM _____

1	2	3	4	5	6	7	8	9	10
11	12	13	14	15	16	17	18	19	20
21	22	23	24	25	26	27	28	29	30
31	32	33	34	35	36	37	38	39	40
41	42	43	44	45	46	47	48	49	50
51	52	53	54	55	56	57	58	59	60
61	62	63	64	65	66	67	68	69	70
71	72	73	74	75	76	77	78	79	80
81	82	83	84	85	86	87	88	89	90
91	92	93	94	95	96	97	98	99	100

GOAL SHOOTER
ATTEMPTS:
SCORED:

GOAL ATTACK
ATTEMPTS:
SCORED:

Should the umpires disagree with the scorers they call for time while both umpires and scorers consult the score sheet.

Since the Code of Rules prescribes that the umpires shall control the game and make decisions they must therefore accept their responsibility and 'call' each centre pass after a goal at their goal end.

This does not prevent the umpires from asking the scorers before the game to advise them after each goal of whose centre pass it is.

Different forms of visual score are used, but those people operating them must be in close contact with the official scorers.

Hints to Scorers

The international sample score sheet must be used for international matches, but some associations print a simpler one for other matches.

Where a score sheet asks for attempts at goal to be recorded, you must be able to interpret the word 'attempts'.

An attempt is recorded when a shot at goal is missed. A shot at goal intercepted by a Goal Defence, or Goalkeeper, who has been penalised for contact or obstruction, is not considered an 'attempt'. However, it is reckoned an attempt when a shooter elects to shoot when awarded a penalty pass in the goal circle but fails to score.

Timekeeper

There shall be an official timekeeper who shall sit at the scoring table.

a. She should be supplied with a stop-watch.
b. She shall take time (start the watch) when the game is started by the umpire's whistle.
c. The *timekeeper* shall signal the end of each quarter (or half), to the nearer umpire by moving to her side and counting down aloud the last five seconds of play.
   In this way the umpire is able to keep her eyes on the game, listen to the count-down and blow her whistle after the last second.
d. Take time when instructed by the umpire who shall blow the whistle to stop play. To restart play the umpire shall signal to the timekeeper and blow the whistle for play to be resumed.
e. Ensure that when instructed by the umpire, time lost for an accident or any other cause is played in the quarter or half in which the stoppage occurred.

The scorers each with a score sheet to mark shall sit at a table with the timekeeper.

The table is best put outside the side line opposite the centre circle, leaving room for the umpire to move along the side line and outside the court.

They should not sit among spectators and should not allow anyone to approach them. Keeping a score sheet or time accurately is a task which requires total concentration.

The timekeeper shall use a stop-watch, preferably with a 'time out' mechanism; a watch with a second hand is not accurate enough.

On verbal instruction from the umpire she shall take 'time out' when the umpire has to stop the game for injury, illness or any other reason. She shall add the amount of time lost to the quarter or half in which a stoppage has occurred.

Captains

The captain is in charge of her team. Her responsibilities include:

1. The toss for choice of goal or first centre pass.
2. To notify the umpire as to which team is to have first centre pass and into which goal her team is shooting.
3. To notify the umpires, and also the opposing captain, if she wishes to change the positions of the players. This is allowed but only during an interval (quarter or half) or after stoppage for injury or illness. The consent of the opposing captain is not necessary.

The captain is also permitted:

a. *to approach an umpire during an interval or after the game for clarification of any rule;*
b. *to thank the umpires after the match;*
c. *during an interval to appeal to the umpire for extra time to deal with an emergency affecting a member of the team and if the appeal is granted to notify the opposing captain of the amount of time that is to be added to the interval.*

Captains should note the new ruling on late arrivals (see below).

The penalty for 3 above is a free pass awarded the first time a player enters an area which was offside in relation to that player's previous playing area. This pass shall be taken from the place in the offside area where the infringement occurred by a player allowed in that area, and after time has been allowed for the captain of the other team to rearrange playing positions if so wished.

The Toss

It is usual for the captains of the two opposing teams to meet the umpires, then for the home captain to toss a coin giving the visiting captain the call.

The captain winning the toss may choose:

(a) to have first centre pass; or
(b) which goal her team will attack ('choice of ends').

If she chooses (a) the other captain has choice of ends.

Before the toss each captain should consult her team as to whether they prefer to choose first centre pass or end. It is most often a definite advantage to choose first centre pass. There are, however, several points to be considered before the decision is made. Notice should be taken of the position of the sun with regard to goal posts, remembering that the sun sinks during the afternoon and might shine in the eyes of the players shooting; the force and direction of the wind; the

personal likes and dislikes of the shooters. On certain occasions, therefore, it might be an advantage to 'choose ends'.

Rule 4

The Team

A team shall consist of seven players.

The game is designed for single sex competition, i.e. a mixed team of men and women is not allowed.

The playing positions are:

Goal Shooter	(GS)
Goal Attack	(GA)
Wing Attack	(WA)
Centre	(C)
Wing Defence	(WD)
Goal Defence	(GD)
Goal Keeper	(GK)

No team may take the court with fewer than five players.

Rule 5

Late Arrivals

1. No player, arriving after play has started, is allowed to replace a player who has filled the position of the late-

comer. Late arrivals may not enter the game while play is in progress.

2. After notifying the umpires she may take the court:
   (a) after a goal has been scored (in this case she must play only in a position left vacant in her team);
   (b) immediately following an interval;
   (c) after a stoppage for injury or illness.

In the case of (b) and (c) the players may change positions so that the late-comer may move to her own place in the team. (See *Captains*, page 13.)

The penalty for breaking rule 2(b) or (c) shall be a free pass to the opposing team where the infringer was standing, and the infringer shall leave the court until the next goal is scored, or until after the next interval.

Rule 6

Substitution

1. *Substitution on court is allowed for up to three players in any one game in the event of injury, illness, or during an interval. At the time a substitution is made playing positions may be changed.*
2. *It is the responsibility of the team captain to notify the umpire and the opposing captain if substitutions and/or changes in playing positions are made.*
3. *Sufficient time shall be allowed for the opposing team to make substitutions and/or changes in playing positions if desired.*

4. *If a substitute is played the original player may take no further part in the game.*

Players who change positions must remember to exchange their bibs, i.e. initials of their playing positions.

Penalty for 6.2

A free pass shall be awarded the first time a player enters an area which was offside in relation to her previous playing area. This pass shall be taken:

(a) from the place in the offside area where the infringement occurred;
(b) by a player allowed in that area;
(c) after time has been allowed for the captain of the other team to re-arrange playing positions if so wished.

The player concerned shall be permitted to remain in the position now being played.

Rule 7

Stoppages, Injuries and Illness

When a player is injured or ill or is unable to continue as a result of any other emergency, a stoppage of up to five minutes is allowed after which it must be decided whether the player is fit to resume play. This decision is left to the team's officials, and not to the umpire.

Play may be stopped by an umpire for an emergency relating to:

(a) equipment, court, weather or interference by outside agencies;

(b) a player's person or clothing;

(c) officials officiating for the match.

The player who is injured, or her captain, must notify the umpire, who shall blow her whistle to stop play, and also signal to the timekeeper to take time out.

The umpire shall decide the length of time for the stoppage and shall ensure that play is re-started as soon as possible.

The timekeeper restarts her watch when the teams are ready to restart play and she receives a signal from the umpire.

Restarting the game after a stoppage

If the game is stopped for an accident it is restarted from the spot at which the ball was when the umpire blew the whistle to stop play. That is to say, the player who was in possession of the ball when play ceased makes her throw and the game continues.

If the ball was out of court, the game is restarted by a throw-in.

If the ball was on the ground when play stopped, or if the umpire does not know who had the ball, then the game is restarted by a toss-up between any two opponents who are allowed in the area, taken on, or as near as possible to, the spot where the ball was when play ceased.

a. During a stoppage for injury or illness, all other players shall remain on court.

b. During this stoppage coaching is not permitted.

c. *After injury or illness when no substitution is made for a player unable to resume play the injured or sick player may return to the vacant position after notifying an umpire of her intention to return to the game.*

SECTION TWO:
Playing Areas
Rule 8

Players are allowed to play only in the following areas:

Goal Shooter in areas 1, 2
Goal Attack   in areas 1, 2, 3
Wing Attack   in areas   2, 3
Centre   in areas   2, 3, 4
Wing Defence in areas   3, 4
Goal Defence in areas   3, 4, 5
Goal Keeper in areas   4, 5

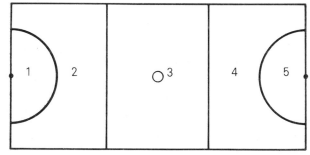

Lines bounding each area are included as part of that area.

It should be noted that Goal Shooter and Goal Keeper may not enter the centre third.

Goal Attack and Goal Defence use two thirds of the court.

Wing Attack and Wing Defence use the centre third and only one goal third—minus the circle.

Centre uses the whole court except the goal circles. Five players only are allowed in the centre third.

Rule 9

Offside

A player is offside if she enters any area other than her playing area. To enter an area means to over-run into it, cross a section of it, or to touch with any part of her body the ground beyond the line which bounds the offside area and her playing area. (See Fig. 1)

If she is on the line but not over at all, then she is not offside. The offside rule is in the nature of 'forbidden territory'; therefore, it makes no difference if a player is in possession of the ball or not.

Providing she does not touch the ground in doing so, a player may reach over and take the ball from an offside area (see Fig. 2), or she may lean on the ball provided no body contact is made with the ground.

GD is offside on attacking court

Attacking court

Defence

Goal

Fig. 1

Fig. 2

Penalty

A free pass to the opposing team, taken from where the player was offside in the forbidden area. The pass must be taken by someone allowed in the area; this means that a player's own opponent may never take the free pass.

Simultaneous offside

When two opposing players, not necessarily opponents, go offside at the same moment:

(i)   If neither makes any contact with the ball—they are not penalised—no whistle. Play continues.
(ii) If one of the two players involved is in possession of the ball or touches it; or
(iii) If both of the two players involved are in possession of the ball or touch it,

a toss-up is given between these two players in their own area of play.

Note (ii) and (iii) suppose that there is an area common to both in which the toss-up can be given, e.g. Red C and Blue WD enter the goal circle at the same time, both having caught the ball. Although the goal circle is offside territory for both, the goal third outside the circle is common, and the toss-up is given in the goal third, opposite the place where they breached the line.

(iv)　If one player allowed only in the goal third goes offside into the centre third, and an opposing player at the same moment goes offside into the goal third, one or both in contact with the ball, then the toss-up is given in the centre third between any two opposing players allowed in that area.

Rule 10

Out of Court

(a) As soon as the ball goes out of play the umpire blows her whistle. The ball is out of court:

(i)　when it touches the ground outside the court;
(ii)　when it touches an object or person in contact with the ground outside the court;
(iii)　when it is held by a player in contact with the ground, an object or a person outside the court.

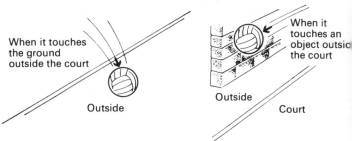

When it touches the ground outside the court

Outside

When it touches an object outside the court

Outside

Court

Penalty for 10(a)

A throw-in to the team opposing the one which last had contact with the ball to be taken where the ball crossed the line.

(b)　A ball which hits any part of the goalpost and rebounds into play is not out of court.

(c)　A player in contact with the ball is out of court when:
(i)　the ground outside the court is touched;
(ii)　any object or person outside the court is touched.

(d)　A player having no contact with the ball may stand or move out of court. However, before she plays the ball she must re-enter the court and have no contact with the ground out of court.

Penalty for 10(c) and 10(d)

A throw-in to the opposing team where the ball crossed the line.

(e)　Defending actions may only be attempted by players standing on court or jumping from court.

When it is held by a player in contact with the ground outside the court

Court

Outside

Penalty for 10(e)

Penalty pass, or penalty pass or shot opposite the spot where the infringer attempted to defend.

(f)　If the ball is caught simultaneously by two opposing players, one of whom lands out of court, a toss-up is taken on court between those two players opposite the point at which the player was out of court.
This phrase 'one of whom lands out of court' does *not* imply that while one player is in contact with the ground outside the court, she may catch the ball—even if it is simultaneously with another. The wording implies that two opposing players on court have jumped and caught

the ball simultaneously while in the air; one lands from the jump inside and the other outside the court; in this case a toss-up is given between these two players on the court opposite the point at which the player was out of court.

(g)　A player who has left the court to retrieve a ball or to take a throw-in must be permitted to re-enter the court directly.

Penalty for 10(g)

Penalty pass, or penalty pass or shot to the opposing team where the infringement occurred.

SECTION THREE:
Conduct of the Game
Rule 11
Positioning of Players for Start of Play

a.　The Centre in possession of the ball shall stand with both feet within the centre circle.

b.　The opposing Centre shall be in the centre third and free to move in that third, but may not take up a close position to the Centre with the ball within three feet from the foot or feet of the Centre.

19

c. All other players shall be in the goal third, which is part of their playing area, and shall be free to move.

Players do not need to stand still and position themselves behind the line. There is opportunity here for the attacking team to experiment and use their initiative and skill to mask their intentions and outwit their opponents.

d. No player, other than the two Centres, is allowed in the centre third until the whistle has been blown to start the game.

Positioning of players for start of play

Penalty

a. If one player enters the centre third before the whistle is blown, a free pass is given to the opposing team where the entry occurred.

b. When any two opposing players simultaneously enter the centre third before the whistle has been blown:

(i) if neither makes contact with the ball they are not penalised and play continues;

(ii) if one of them touches or catches the ball a toss-up is taken between these two players near to where the infringement occurred.

Rule 12

Start of Play

1. (i) The umpire shall blow her whistle to start and restart play.

(ii) The pass made by a Centre in response to the umpire's whistle at the start and restart of play shall be designated a centre pass.

(iii) Play shall be started and restarted after each goal is scored, and after each interval, by a centre pass taken alternately by the two Centres throughout the game.

(iv) If, at a centre pass, the ball is still in the Centre's hands when the umpire's whistle is blown to signal the end of a quarter or half that team will therefore take the pass after the interval.

2. (i) When the whistle is blown the Centre in possession of the ball shall throw it within three seconds and shall obey the Footwork Rule.

(ii) The centre pass shall be caught or touched by any other player who is standing or who lands within the centre third.
A player who lands with the first foot, or on both feet simultaneously, wholly within the centre third is judged to have received the ball in that third. That

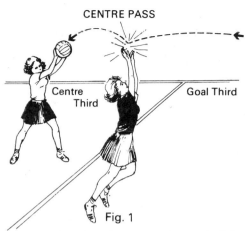

CENTRE PASS

Centre Third   Goal Third

Fig. 1

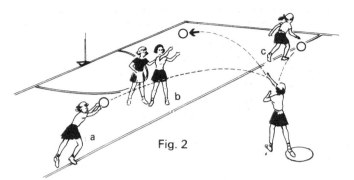

Fig. 2

player's subsequent throw shall be considered to have been made from the centre third (see Fig. 1).

A player who lands on both feet simultaneously, with one foot wholly within the centre third and the other wholly within the goal third, is judged to have received the ball in the goal third (see Fig. 2a, c).

(iii) If a member of the team taking the centre pass catches the ball in the goal third without having touched it in the centre third, a free pass shall be awarded to the opposing team, to be taken in the goal third close to the point where the ball crossed the line (see Fig. 2b).

(iv) If a member of the opposing team touches or catches the centre pass in the centre third or in the goal third, or with feet astride the transverse line, play shall continue (see Fig 3).

(v) If the ball from the centre pass goes untouched over the side line bounding the centre third, a throw-in is awarded to the opposing team where the ball crossed the line.

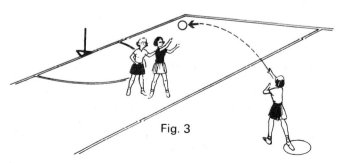

Fig. 3

Rule 13

Playing the Ball

1. A player may:
   - (i) catch the ball with one or both hands;
   - (ii) gain or regain control of the ball if it rebounds from the goalpost (this includes the ring);
   - (iii) bat or bounce to another player a ball that comes within her reach, without first having possession of it;
   - (iv) tip the ball in an uncontrolled manner once or more than once and then:
     - (a) catch the ball; or
     - (b) direct the ball to another player;
   - (v) having batted the ball once, either catch the ball or direct it to another player;
   - (vi) having bounced the ball once, either catch the ball or direct the ball to another player;
   - (vii) roll the ball to oneself to gain possession;
   - (viii) fall while holding the ball, but must regain footing and throw within three seconds of receiving the ball;
   - (ix) lean on the ball to prevent going offside;
   - (x) lean on the ball on court to gain balance;
   - (xi) jump from a position in contact with the court and play the ball outside the court, provided that neither the player nor the ball make contact with the ground, or any object or person outside the court while the ball is being played.

2. A player may not:
   - (i) deliberately kick the ball (a ball which is thrown and accidentally hits the leg of a player is not deemed to be a kick);
   - (ii) strike the ball with a fist;
   - (iii) deliberately fall on the ball to get it;
   - (iv) attempt to gain possession of the ball while lying, sitting or kneeling on the ground;
   - (v) throw the ball while lying, sitting, or kneeling on the ground;
   - (vi) use the goalpost as a support in recovering a ball going out of court;
   - (vii) use the goalpost as a means of regaining balance, or in any other way for any other purpose.

Penalty

Free pass to the opposing team where the infringement occurred.

3. When a player has caught or held the ball she shall play it or shoot for goal within three seconds.

To play the ball a player may:
   - (i) throw it in any manner and in any direction to another player;
   - (ii) bounce it with one or both hands in any direction to another player.

4. When a player has caught or held the ball she may not:
   - (i) roll the ball to another player;

(ii) throw the ball and play it before it has been touched by another player;

(iii) toss the ball into the air and replay it;

(iv) drop the ball and replay it; (This needs clarifying: if the player has held the ball so that she could have thrown it, then drops and catches it again, she has replayed the ball. However, if the ball touches and passes through her hands and then she catches it, she has not replayed the ball.)

(v) bounce the ball and replay it;

(vi) *replay the ball after an unsuccessful shot at goal unless it has touched some part of the goalpost or ring.*

Penalty for 4

Free pass to the opposing team where the infringement occurred.

Passing Distances

5. Short pass
(i) On the court: at the moment the ball is passed there must be room for a third player to move between *the hands* of the thrower and those of the receiver to try to intercept the ball.

(ii) At the throw-in: at the moment the ball is passed there must be room on the court between *the hands* of the thrower and those of the receiver for a third player to attempt an interception.

Off Court

Penalty

Free pass to the opposing team where the ball was caught.

Throwing Over a Third

The ball may not be thrown over a complete third without being touched or caught by a player who at the time of touching or catching the ball is wholly within that third. This means that the ball may not cross two transverse lines untouched, i.e.

(a) from behind the goal line into centre third;
(b) from goal third into the other goal third;
(c) from centre third out of court behind goal line.

A player who lands with her first foot **wholly** within the correct third is deemed to have received the ball in that third, and her subsequent throw to have been made from that third.

A player who lands on both feet simultaneously with parts of

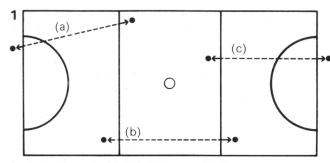

both feet in each third shall be penalised.

1. Ball thrown over complete third of court.
    (a) Ball thrown from behind goal line received in centre third.
    (b) Ball thrown from goal third received in other goal third
    (c) Ball thrown from centre third received behind goal third

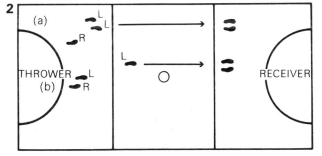

2. Two examples of ball thrown over complete third of court looking at thrower.
    (a) Completely behind line for catch and throw.
    (b) Catch behind line, step into next third with throw.

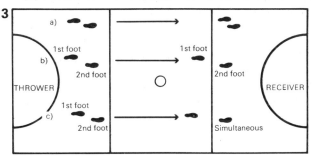

3. Two examples of throwing over a complete third, looking at the receiver, and (b), a correct throw.
    (a) Wrong   (b) Correct.   (c) Wrong.

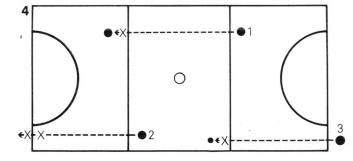

4. Penalty for throwing over complete third. X shows where free pass is taken for throwing over a complete third.

A player who lands on both feet simultaneously, with one foot wholly within the correct third and the other in the incorrect third, shall be penalised.

Penalty

Free pass to the opposing team taken just beyond the second line that the ball has crossed except where the ball thrown from the centre third passes out of court over the goal line, when a throw-in shall be taken.

Rule 14

Footwork

A player has freedom in her throwing movements to encourage a better use of body weight to produce greater accuracy of direction and force and to allow a follow-through to a throw. The permitted movement of the feet starts when a player has gained control of the ball. The ball may be received while the player has one or both feet on the ground, or while she is in the air in a jump. In the latter case the player could land with the ball from her jump on to one foot or on to both feet simultaneously. The following is an analysis of the allowed movement of the feet in these two alternatives:

A. If a player receives the ball while one foot is grounded, or jumps to catch and lands on one foot, she may then:

(i) Step with the other foot in any direction and lift the landing foot and throw or shoot before this foot is regrounded.

(ii) Step with the other foot in any direction any number of times, pivoting on the landing foot. The pivoting foot

A(i)

may be lifted but the player must throw or shoot before regrounding it.

(iii) Jump from the landing foot onto the other foot and jump again but must throw the ball before regrounding either foot. A considerable amount of ground can be covered in this movement if a leap forward is made to catch, another leap forward from first landing foot for second, and a third leap from this foot—the ball, of course, must be thrown while the player is still in the air during this last leap.

A(ii)

(iv) Step with the other foot and jump from it but must throw the ball before regrounding either foot. (Dragging or sliding of the landing foot and hopping on either foot are not allowed.)

B. If a player receives the ball while both feet are grounded, or jumps to catch and lands on both feet simultaneously, she may then:

(i) Step with either foot in any direction, lift the other foot and throw or shoot before this foot is regrounded.

(ii) Step with either foot in any direction any number of times pivoting on the other. The pivoting foot may be lifted but the player must throw or shoot before regrounding it.

(iii) Jump from both feet onto either foot, but must throw or shoot before regrounding the other foot.

(iv) Step with either foot, and jump, but must throw the ball before regrounding either foot.

A player in possession of the ball may not:

(i) Drag or slide the landing foot.

(ii) Hop on either foot.

(iii) Jump from both feet and land on both feet unless the ball has been released before landing.

Penalty

A free pass to the opposing team where the infringement occurred.

C. Footwork for the taking of penalties

At a free pass, penalty pass, shot and throw-in the Footwork Rule as in A(i), (ii), (iii), (iv) is applied. This is as though the foot placed on the spot or at the point immediately behind the line where the infringement occurred and immediately behind the point where the ball crossed the line at a throw-in were equivalent to the landing foot in a one-foot landing. It may also be equivalent to receiving the ball with one foot grounded before throwing or shooting. Therefore a player must place one foot at the spot indicated by the umpire. This foot may be used only to pivot, or it may be lifted.

Note for umpires

Much practice is needed to detect inaccurate footwork quickly. It is not safe to go by the number of sounds made by the feet on touching the ground. The Umpire must watch the foot which lands first after the player receives or has control of the ball. The foot which lands first may not be lifted or jumped from and then be grounded a second time while the ball is still held.

Penalty—Free pass to opposing team, where the infringement occurred.

When the game has been stopped for an infringement and the penalty is awarded, the umpire starts timing the 3 seconds from the moment the player taking the penalty has the ball in her possession at the correct place.

Catching

1. Two-handed catch

Arms should be stretched towards the ball, fingers opened. As the ball comes into the hands the whole arm and body must 'give' in the direction of the flight of the ball so that the catch is 'soft' and almost noiseless. If the hands and arms are rigid, one is liable to damage fingers.

The management of the feet when catching is important. If right-handed, always try to land on the **right foot**, in a one-two landing.

2. One-handed catch

Simple to learn if the above rules are applied about 'giving'. The advantage is that a player can extend her reach by using one hand only.

Throwing

1. Chest pass

The fingers of both hands are spread behind the ball which is held close to the chest. By an elbow, wrist and finger push, the ball is pushed from both hands. Used for a short quick pass.

Chest Throw (A)   Chest Throw (B)

2. Straight shoulder pass

The hand should be spread out behind the ball with the whole body turned sideways and the weight on the back foot. The throwing arm is thrust forward from the elbow and shoulder with follow-through of body weight and the hips turned forward as the ball is released. A final flick of the wrist will give speed to the flight of the ball.

This pass should be directed on to the free side of the player, beyond her, in the direction she is moving. The distance ahead will depend on the speed of the runner.

This is the most-used pass where length and power is needed. With a right-handed throw the left foot should be forward to balance the body.

3a. High shoulder pass

This is like the last pass but the weight must be behind and below the ball to direct it in an upward direction over the head of the opponent.

3b. Bounce pass

This is as above, but the weight must be behind and on top of the ball to direct it downwards.

4. Underarm pass

The action here is like that of shovelling. The flight of the ball is waist high or lower and direct. It is only used for a very short pass. The ball travels very fast.

Players must use their ingenuity when throwing. With the possibility of an opponent standing only 0.9 metres (3 feet) away, waiting to intercept the pass, the thrower must select passes, 1, 2, 3 or 4 illustrated, or bounce the ball to another player, or adapt her action in order to avoid interception.

5. Two-handed overhead pass

The ball is held in two hands behind the head, and then flicked up to lift the ball over an opponent's head. Similar action to a soccer 'throw-in'. (see over)

Overhead two handed throw

Getting Free

To 'get free', that is, to shake off an opponent, a player can:

(i)   Get behind her opponent so that she is unsighted, make a decided feint move to one side and then spring in the opposite direction, i.e. a feint move to the right and a sprint to the left, stretching out the left hand to indicate that she wants the ball on that side of her.

(ii)   Feint in a backward direction and sprint forwards to meet the ball and receive a short pass

(iii) Feint forwards, and run backwards to receive a high pass over her opponent's head. This is the least effective move since a high-looped pass is always more easily intercepted.

(iv) Suddenly sprint either from a stationary position or from a gentle walk or run into a space. This is only attempted if the player is a fast runner or has a good sprint start.

(v)   Sprint in the direction she wishes to go and stop suddenly. The ball in this case must be carefully aimed on the catcher's free side.

Similar moves must be made against an opponent marking with the object of preventing an attacker from moving into an area where she wants the ball.

Marking

Marking is the effort a player makes to prevent her opponent from receiving the ball.

The marker should follow her opponent closely the whole time her team is in possession of the ball and endeavour always to keep between her and the ball.

It is a mistake to allow the dodger to get directly behind because the marker is then completely unsighted. She should be able to see both her and the ball with a quick turn of the head. It is most essential to watch the ball at all times and leave the opponent and go for the ball whenever the opportunity occurs.

Although the aim of a defending player is to gain possession of the ball, there are occasions when it might be of greater advantage to her team if the player defends her opponent in such a way as to try to prevent her from moving into an area

where she can use the ball with greater advantage to her team.

In this case the marker should place herself between her opponent and the area into which she wishes to move. She then face marks in an endeavour to cut off her opponent's pathway. She should try to keep squarely in front of her attacker as she dodges to create the space to get through.

Intercepting

If a player has failed to prevent her opponent from receiving the ball she should recover quickly and move in front of her opponent to attempt to intercept her pass or shot for goal.

She is not penalised if the thrower or shooter jumps forward or steps forward.

Having gauged her distance or taken up her position, the defender should assume a 'gathered in' stance from which she can spring upwards or to the side to reach the greatest possible height. In intercepting a shot, as much use must be taken of spring and stretch for the interception to be successful. There should be one all-out effort to get the ball. **She must make her spring a moment before the ball leaves the shooter's hands.** If she jumps too soon she may recover, move back and make a second attempt if time permits. **She should jump forwards to take the ball as soon as it leaves the shooter's hands.**

Defenders may *not* substitute for this effort *any* movement or stance which might be interpreted as intimidating the shooter to 'put her off' her aim or concentration. This is obstruction. One can also assume a stance side-ways to the shooter and thrust one arm up to intercept. The 0.9 metre (3 feet) distance applies in the same way.

Shooters must vary their style of shooting to avoid interception, and use the stationary aimed shot only when near the post.

A defender does not have to remain upright; her hands may be held forward, so long as she does not contact her opponent or the ball.

Rule 15

Scoring a Goal

A goal is scored when the ball is thrown or batted over and completely through the ring into the net by Goal Shooter or Goal Attack from any point within the goal circle including the lines bounding the circle.

(i)   If any player other than Goal Shooter or Goal Attack throws the ball through the ring no goal is scored and play continues.

(ii) If a defending player deflects a shot for goal and the ball then passes over and completely through the ring the goal is scored.

(iii) Goal Shooter or Goal Attack may shoot for goal or pass if the ball **is won at a toss-up** in the goal circle.

(iv) If the whistle for an interval or 'time' is blown before the ball has passed **completely** through the ring, the goal is not scored.

(v)   If the whistle for an interval or 'time' is blown **after** a penalty pass or shot has been awarded to Goal Shooter or Goal Attack in the goal circle, a penalty shot shall be completed.

Taking a Shot for Goal

In taking a shot for goal a player shall:

(i)   Have no contact with the ground outside the goal circle either during the catching of the ball or while she is holding it. It is not contact with the ground to balance on the ball, but if this happens behind the goal line the ball is considered to be out of court. If she jumps, makes her catch and lands with one foot in and one outside the circle, or lands and then places the other outside to gain her balance, she may not shoot.

As soon as she attempts to shoot in these cases, she is penalised. Remember that it is having part of her body outside the circle, whether it be hand or foot, and then attempting to shoot that is the infringement. *Therefore the penalty is taken from where she attempted to shoot.*

Since it is the shooter's feet, or any part of her which counts, she is not penalised if, being completely in the circle, but unbalanced, she leans on the ball on the ground outside the circle, in the goal third. (see over)

(iii) Obey the Footwork Rule
A shooter cannot force her opponent out of the way in order to step or jump. Readers need to study both the Footwork Rule and the Obstruction Rule to know what is permitted.

Penalty

A free pass to the opposing team in the goal circle where the infringement occurred.

If a defending player causes the goalpost to move so as to interfere with the shot at goal, a penalty pass or shot shall be awarded to the opposing team.

If the infringer was out of court, the penalty shall be taken on court near the place where the infringer was standing.

Rule 16

Obstruction

An attempt to intercept or defend the ball *may* be made by a defending player if the distance on the ground is not less than 0.9 metres (3 feet) from a player in possession of the ball. When the ball is received, this distance is measured as follows:

(i) if the player's landing, grounded or pivoting foot remains on the ground, the distance is measured from that foot to the nearer foot of the defending player;

(ii) Shoot within three seconds of catching or holding the ball.
Many shooters extend the three seconds limit by catching, making a pivot, lifting the ball to aim, and making feint movements to avoid a defending opponent before releasing the ball—it is difficult to go through all these motions within three seconds; even to catch, lean on the ball, stand up and shoot takes time.

(ii)   if the player's landing, grounded or pivoting foot is lifted, the distance is measured from the spot on the ground from which the foot was lifted, to the nearer foot of the defending player;

Not less than 0.9 m (3 ft)

0.9 m (3 ft)

(iii)   if the player is standing or lands on both feet simultaneously and remains grounded on both feet, the distance is measured from whichever is the nearer foot of that player to the nearer foot of the defending player;

(iv)   if the player is standing or lands on both feet simultaneously and either foot is lifted, the other foot is considered to be the grounded foot from which the 0.9 m (3 ft) distance is measured.

From the correct distance, a defending player *may* attempt to intercept or defend the ball:

(i)   by jumping towards the player with the ball, but if the landing is within 0.9 m (3 ft) of that player and interferes with the throwing or shooting motion, obstruction occurs;

(ii)   if the player with the ball steps forward to lessen the distance of 0.9 m (3 ft) between them.

A player *may* be within 0.9 m (3 ft) of an opponent in possession of the ball providing no effort is made to defend and there is no interference with that opponent's throwing or shooting action.

From the correct distance, a defending player *may not* attempt to intercept or defend the ball by stepping towards an opponent with the ball.

Obstruction of a player not in possession of the ball

A player is obstructing if within a distance of 0.9 m (3 ft) (measured on the ground) from an opponent without the ball, any movements are employed by that player (whether attacking or defending) which take the arms away from the body, other than those involved in natural body balance. Within this distance a player is not obstructing if the arms are outstretched:

(i) to catch, deflect or intercept a pass or feint pass;
(ii) to obtain a rebound from an unsuccessful shot at goal;
(iii) momentarily to signal for a pass, or to indicate the intended direction of movement

Obstruction by intimidation

When a player with or without the ball intimidates an opponent it is obstruction.

Penalty

Penalty pass or penalty pass or shot where the infringer is standing except where this places the non-offending team at a disadvantage, when the penalty shall be taken where the obstructed player was standing.

Defending a player who is out of court

A player may defend an opponent who has chosen to go out of court provided that the defending player does not leave the court or own playing area in order to defend.

Penalty

A penalty pass or penalty pass or shot on court immediately opposite the point at which the obstruction occurred.

Obstruction by a player from out of court

A player who is standing out of court may not attempt to defend a player who is on the court.

Penalty

A penalty pass or penalty pass or shot on the court opposite the point at which the defending player is standing.

Rule 17

Contact

1. Personal contact

No player shall come into personal contact with an opponent in such a manner as to interfere with her play either accidentally or deliberately.

(i) By her own effort to get free she shall not:
    (a) push her opponent in any way;
    (b) trip or knock her opponent in any way.

(ii) By her own effort to contact the ball she shall not throw her body against an opponent or rush into her. (see over)

(iii) By her effort to defend, she shall not:
    (a) keep her elbow against an opponent;
    (b) hold an opponent (this includes feeling to keep near her);
    (c) push an opponent;
    (d) charge an opponent, that is, when jumping, throw her body against a player.

(iv) Whether attempting to get free, or to defend, a player is responsible for any personal contact if:

(a) she takes a position so near an opponent that contact is inevitable;

(b) if she takes a position so quickly into a moving opponent's path that contact cannot be avoided.

(a)

(b)

Contact would be inevitable when an opponent places her body or part of her body in such a position that the original mover is unable to avoid contact, e.g. a foot thrust out, knee swivelling, shoulder jutted out, chest thrust forward. A player who has begun a movement, a sudden dart, or a jump, cannot stop to avoid the opponent who moves suddenly into her pathway.

A player shall not contact another on any other occasion or in any other way in such a manner as to interfere with her play.

Defending by keeping an elbow against an opponent

2. Contact with the ball

(i)   A player while holding the ball shall not touch or push an opposing player with it in such a manner as to interfere with her play.

Contact with the ball

(ii) A player shall not place a hand or hands on, or remove from her possession, the ball held by an opposing player either accidentally or deliberately.

(ii) Where (i) and (ii) occur simultaneously a toss-up is given between the two players.

The umpire now has an added responsibility. Whereas the umpire usually said 'Blue's ball' if Red's hands were second on the ball, now Blue is given a penalty pass for 'contact'.

Penalty

The penalty for (i) and (ii) is a penalty pass or shot where the infringer is standing, except where this places the non-offending team at a disadvantage when the penalty shall be taken where the contacted player was standing.

SECTION FOUR: **Penalties**

The penalties awarded for the breaking of the rules are:

1. The free pass.
2. The penalty pass or shot.
3. The throw-in.
4. the toss-up.

General Rules for the Taking of Penalties

1. A penalty for an infringement of the rules on court is taken where the infringement occurred except:
   (a) where the *advantage rule* applies, i.e. the umpire shall refrain from blowing the whistle to penalise an infringement when by so doing the non-offending team would be placed at a disadvantage;
   (b) as provided for under Penalty for Rules 16 and 17, Obstruction and Contact.
2. The umpire indicates the correct place. (The umpire may enter the court to point to the correct place.)

3. The penalties, with the exception of the toss-up, are awarded to a team. Providing she is allowed in the area where the penalty is awarded, any member of the opposing team may take the penalty.
4. The player taking the penalty must throw the ball within three seconds after she has taken up her position at the correct place and being in possession of the ball.
5. In the taking of a free pass, penalty pass or shot or throw-in, the Footwork Rule applies as though the foot placed at the point indicated were equivalent to the landing foot in a one-foot landing, or to receiving the ball with one foot grounded. (See the Footwork Rule.)
6. If a player taking a free pass, or penalty pass or shot, infringes 3–5 above, a free pass is awarded to the opposing team.
7. If a player taking a throw-in infringes 3–5 above, a throw-in is awarded to the opposing team.

Free Pass

1. A free pass is awarded for infringements of the rules on the court, with the exception of the Rules of Contact and Obstruction, simultaneous offences by two opposing players and interference with the goal post.
2. When a free pass is awarded, the ball may be thrown by any player in the opposing team allowed in the area, but the ball may not be thrown over a complete third of the court without being touched or caught by a player in that third.

Penalty Pass

1. A penalty pass, or a penalty pass shot is awarded for infringement of the Rules of Contact and Obstruction.

Obstruction at a penalty pass

2. A player penalised for Obstruction and Contact must stand beside and away from the thrower taking the penalty and must make no attempt to take part in the play until the ball has left the thrower's hands. If the infringer moves before the ball has left the thrower's hands the penalty shall be retaken unless the pass or shot is successful.

Explanation. Offenders in the past have often stood so close to the player taking the pass or shot that the action

becomes inhibited. To avoid this disadvantage to the thrower, the offender may stand either side of the thrower but beside, which means 'at the side of', and 'level' with the thrower and must stand 'away' from her. No distance is specified but must be such that the thrower has freedom to make the type of pass or shot she wants.

3. The penalty shall be taken from where the infringer was standing, except where this puts the non-offending team at a disadvantage, when the penalty shall be taken where the obstructed or contacted player was standing.

4. Any player allowed in the area may take the penalty.

5. (i) An attempt to intercept the penalty pass or shot may be made by any opposing player other than the offender.
   (ii) If an opponent obstructs or contacts the thrower during the taking of the penalty pass or shot, a penalty pass or shot shall be awarded at the spot where the second infringer was standing unless this places the non-offending team at a disadvantage.
   (iii) Both the original and second offenders must stand beside and away from the thrower taking the penalty and make no attempt to take part in the play until the ball has left the thrower's hands.

6. When two members of a team simultaneously obstruct or contact a member of the opposing team, each offender shall stand beside and away from the thrower taking the penalty. They must make no attempt to take part in the play until the ball has left the thrower's hands.

7. A Goal Shooter or Goal Attack taking a penalty pass in the goal circle may either pass or shoot for goal

Throw-in

1. When it goes out of court the ball shall be put into play by a member of the opposing team, either:
   (i) the player who last had contact with the ball; or
   (ii) the player who received the ball with any part of her touching the ground outside the court

Taking the throw-in

2. The player throwing the ball in shall:
   (i) Stand outside the court and place one foot as close as possible to the line without touching or standing on it, at the point where the Umpire indicates that the ball has crossed the line; (*thrower should stand upright and erect.*)
   (ii) Wait for the umpire to say 'Play!' when all others are on the court.
   (iii) Throw within three seconds after the umpire has called 'Play'.
   (iv) Not enter the court until the ball has left her hands.
   (v) Throw into the nearest third of the court from behind the goal lines or the nearest or adjacent third from behind the side lines.
   (vi) Throw only from behind a line bounding her own playing area. *If using the Footwork Rule the player must remain behind this area until she has released the ball.*
   (vii) Apply the Footwork Rule as in Penalties, General Rules 5 (see page 38).

Note Remember that the one foot placed where the umpire indicates, can only be lifted or pivoted; it may not be used to make a step.

The other foot may be used to take a step sideways or backwards, but not of course, on to the court

Penalties for infringements occurring at the throw-in

1. By the thrower—such as:
   (a) standing back from the line
   (b) standing two feet together, with weight equally distributed
   (c) standing with part of one or both feet touching on or over the line
   (d) not waiting for 'Play!' from the umpire
   (e) tossing the ball, dropping it, etc.
   (f) holding ball for more than three seconds
   (g) stepping behind or beyond a line bounding her area.

—a throw-in is awarded to the opposing team at the spot where the infringement occurred, when the penalty is as for throwing over a third.

2. By a member of the opposing team—if she:
   (a) contacts
   (b) obstructs or intimidates on the court

—a penalty pass is awarded on the court, where the infringement occurred.

3. If the ball fails to enter the court the penalty throw-in shall be taken by the opposing team from the original throw-in point.

4. When the ball from a throw-in goes out of court without being touched, a throw in shall be taken by the opposing team from behind the point at which the ball last went out.

5. If the ball is sent out of court simultaneously by two players in opposing teams, or if the umpire cannot decide who touched the ball last, there shall be a toss-up opposite the point at which the ball went out.

The umpire responsible for decisions with regard to the throw-in, where it occurs along the side line bounding the other umpire's half, awards the penalties for infringements directly concerned with the throw-in as in 2 (above) although they occur on court. If a toss-up is awarded, she will take it.

Toss-up

1. A toss-up puts the ball into play when:
    (i)   opposing players gain simultaneous possession of the ball with either or both hands;
    (ii)   opposing players simultaneously knock the ball out of court;
    (iii) opposing players are involved, and the umpire is unable to determine the last player to touch the ball before it goes out of court;
    (iv)   opposing players are simultaneously offside, one in possession of or touching the ball;
    (v)   opposing players make simultaneous contact which interferes with play;
    (vi)   after an accident the umpires are unable to say who had the ball, or whether the ball was on the ground when play stopped.

Out of Court

Side Line

Where and how the toss-up is taken

The toss-up is taken on court between the two opposing players concerned, as near as possible to the place where the incident occurred.

The two players shall stand facing each other and their own goal ends with arms straight and hands to sides, but feet in any position. There shall be a distance of 0.9 m (3 ft) between the nearer foot of one player and that of her opponent. They shall not move from this position until the whistle is blown. If one player moves too soon, a free pass is awarded to the opposing team.

The umpire shall release the ball midway between the two players from just below shoulder level of the shorter player's normal standing position. Momentarily, the umpire shall be stationary and shall hold the ball in the palm of one hand and shall flick it vertically not more than 600 mm (2 ft) in the air as the whistle is blown.

The ball may be caught, or it may be batted in any direction except directly at the opposing player. All other players may stand or move anywhere within their playing area as long as they do not interfere with the toss-up. Goal Shooter or Goal Attack may shoot for goal or pass if the ball is won at toss-up in the goal circle.

When the toss-up cannot be taken where the incident occurred because of the boundaries involved, the following applies:

(i) where the incident involves two opposing players across a line dividing areas, one of which is common to both players, the toss-up is taken between those two players in the common area;

(ii) where the incident involves two opposing players from adjoining playing areas across a transverse line and no area is common to both, the toss-up is taken in the centre third between any two opposing players allowed in that area;

(iii) when two opposing players simultaneously knock the ball out of court over a line bounding an area which is not common to both, the toss-up is taken between any two opposing players allowed in that area, on court opposite the point at which the ball crossed the line.

SECTION FIVE: **Discipline**

The breaking of rules and/or the employment of any action not covered by the wording of the rules in a manner contrary to the spirit of the game is not permitted.

This includes the breaking of rules:

1. (i) Between the scoring of a goal and the restart of play;

   (ii) Between the ball going out of court and the throw-in;

   (iii) Between the award and taking of any penalty in court.

Penalty for 1

Immediately the play restarts, the umpire shall penalise the infringement unless the non-offending team is placed at a disadvantage.

2. The deliberate delaying of play.

Penalty for 2

Free pass unless the non-offending team is placed at a disadvantage.

3. Deliberate action to prevent a player from re-entering the court after throwing-in or retrieving a ball.

Penalty for 3

Penalty pass or penalty pass or shot where the infringer was standing.

An umpire may:

(i) Order a player to leave the court, but only when sure that the ordinary penalty is insufficient and, except in extreme cases, only after a warning;

(ii) Stand a player off the court for a specified part of the game, e.g. until the next goal is scored, until the next interval or for the rest of the game.

When a player is suspended, that player may not be replaced. In the event of a Centre being suspended, that team may move only ONE player to allow play to continue. That player shall continue to play as Centre until the next interval. At the end of the suspension period the suspended player must return to the vacant position. During playing time an umpire has the right to warn against any coaching from the sidelines and if coaching persists, after due warning, may penalise the team which may benefit.

An umpire can raise the standard of a game by good umpiring. A game played with the wrong spirit is not enjoyable; players who try to find a way 'around the rules', who 'play' the umpire, who defend by trying to prevent an opponent from playing are guilty of playing in the wrong spirit, and make the umpires' task very difficult.

Duties of Umpires

On the court before the game

1. Check the condition of equipment to see:

(i)   If the marking of the court can be improved with chalk, or the surface improved with sweeping.
(ii) if the goal rings need levelling.
(iii) if the goalposts are vertically over the middle point of the goal lines.
(iv) That the ball is of suitable weight and size, and has no dangling lace.

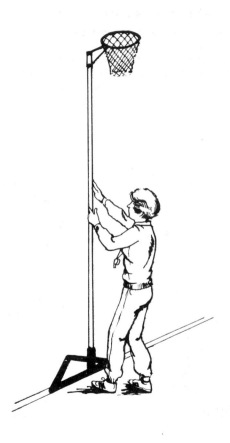

2. Arrange with the other umpire as to which half of the court and which side line each shall control.

3. Arrange who shall blow first whistle.

4. Ascertain the name and distinguishing colours of each team and inform the official scorers.

5. Ascertain which team is taking first centre pass and inform the official scorers.

6. Arrange for time to be kept by an appointed timekeeper.

7. Arrange with the scorers to check, or call the centre pass if required.

Use of whistle

The whistle should be blown firmly and with a short blast.

It should be blown:

(i) To start the game at the beginning of each quarter, and to restart the game after each goal

(ii) To stop play at the end of each quarter, and to end the match.

The umpire must try to restart the game as quickly as possible after the goal has been scored and immediately the players have reached their starting areas; there is no need to wait until all players are stationary and settled. She should see that no players delay the restart by dawdling—time out is not taken for this action.

(iii) To stop the game for an infringement of the rules, when necessary.

Too many umpires blow the whistle for every infringement, which spoils the rhythm of play—they must see the whole game in their half and not just the player with the ball; the Advantage Rule should be played whenever possible. If however, she blows, she must then award the penalty, for the advantage has been lost.

The umpire should hold the whistle in her mouth the whole time that play is in her half of the court. While play is at the other end of the court, the whistle should be held ready in the hand to put to the mouth instantly when the situation demands.

Use of voice

The umpire should speak clearly and loudly enough so that every player can hear her words, for what she has to say affects the farthermost player even if she is at the opposite end of the court.

When the umpire blows her whistle to stop the game for an infringement she shall:

(i)   state the infringement;
(ii) state the penalty and the team to take it;
(iii) indicate the point at which the penalty shall be taken.

When the ball goes out of court she shall:

(i)   blow the whistle to stop the game;
(ii) state the infringement;
(iii) state the penalty and the team to take it;
(iv) indicate the point at which the penalty shall be taken;
(v)   say 'Play!' when all other players are on court.

Appendix

Hand signals may be used to clarify decisions [Rule 3.1 Umpire: Clause 3.1.5. (x)]

Guidelines for appropriate signals are given for some of the rules as follows:

Stepping	– Rolling hands
Distance in obstruction	– Hands apart in front of body
Personal contact	– One hand hits the other
Held ball	– Fingers apart held up
Direction of pass	– Arm pointed towards one goal line
Toss-up	– Palm of hand moved vertically upwards
Take time	– Make a 'T' with the fingers of one hand against the palm of the other.

ALL ENGLAND NETBALL ASSOCIATION LIMITED

The All England Netball Association Ltd governs the game of Netball in England. The A.E.N.A. is affiliated to the International Federation of Netball Associations.

Headquarters

Francis House, Francis Street, London SW1P 1DE

Any enquiries should be addressed to the Director. Queries on Rules of the Game may be addressed to the National Technical Officer. Affiliated members only have this privilege, and when writing should state their membership number.

Publications

The following publications are obtainable from Headquarters

Official Netball Rules	Price £2.00
for affiliated members ...	£1.00
Netball Skills	£1.00
Pick-a-Practice Cards	£1.00

The following are obtainable from A & C Black (Publishers) Ltd, Howard Road, Eaton Socon, Huntingdon, Cambridgeshire, PE19 3EZ

EP Sport Netball by Rena B. Stratford ... ... Price £4.95
The Netball Coaching Manual (the official A.E.N.A. coaching manual) edited by Heather Crouch £8.95

VIDEO FILMS can be hired from the Association

Eligibility for membership—Any school, college or youth club is eligible to become a member. Enquiries should be addressed to the Director.

Printed in England by Swannack, Brown & Co. Ltd., Hull